The Good & Bad About Flipping Houses

SEAN T. DANLEY

The Good & Bad About Flipping Houses

Table of Contents

The Good & Bad About Flipping Houses

PREFACE

I'll begin this book much the same way I ended the preface of my first installment of my Good & Bad book series entitled, "The Good & Bad about Hard Money Lenders." And that's by saying whether you are a newbie or seasoned real estate investor, a first-time homebuyer or seller, I hope you find at least one *"ah ha"* piece of information that might help you on your real estate investment journey.

I am by no means a real estate mogul or guru, but I am a guy who's been involved in the real estate industry since 2004—yep 20 years in various capacities. But my introduction to real estate was long before I knew or understood the value of this asset class. I was born in Los Angeles and raised in Inglewood, California and introduced to the real estate industry by my dad, an Electrician turned real estate broker.

My parents split up when I was eleven, but to the surprise of many, I wasn't raised by a single mom. My dad actually raised me and my two younger siblings while my mom split town for Chicago, where she was born and raised.

Four years later, when I was fifteen, my dad married a schoolteacher whose father just so happened to be Inglewood's first black independent real estate broker, Joseph Mayfield Sr. My stepmom's brother, Joe Jr. was also building his own real estate rental empire by taking the information he'd learned from his father and putting it to use in the form of buying single-family and multi-family properties throughout Los Angeles and Inglewood.

As I look back now, these two men were real-life *millionaires next door* long before the book, because they didn't live in big, fancy houses, drive the latest expensive cars, or flaunt their wealth by any means. They were modest, even frugal to some degree. The thing that stood out to me most was that they didn't punch anyone else's clock! They were full-time entrepreneurs/businessmen and I admired that about them both.

Soon after, my dad, stepmom and her dad partnered on a real estate flip on an old house near the University of Southern California (USC). Remember when I said I was introduced to real estate long before I understood its value? Well, the house, as I remember, was a typical two- or three-bedroom California bungalow, most likely built in the 30's or 40's. Zero curb appeal, the grass was overgrown and there was trash and leftover furnishings scattered about. That's where I came in, because they hired me to clean it out for a few dollars they threw my way for a weekend of work.

It was menial labor, but I'd been doing electrical side jobs with my dad and his brother (a journeyman plumber by trade) since I was a kid. I never liked it much, but I was used to dirty work, as they sent me up a ladder onto to some rooftop, attic, or even down into some filthy crawlspace underneath houses regularly. Hey, I always got paid and what teenage kid doesn't like a few extra dollars

in his or her pocket to blow off frivolously?
I may have seen the fully renovated flip project but can't say I committed it to memory. Because as a kid, I didn't understand the value of some old raggedy house made anew. I know they ended up selling the house a short time later, but don't ask me what the numbers looked like. *You don't know what you don't know*, and at the time (1989 or 1990), I had no idea the potential profits real estate could yield. All I knew was that they made some money on the flip once it sold.

Guaranteed, if that house is still standing today, with all the gentrification that's taken and still taking place throughout Los Angeles and Inglewood; especially near a higher education institution as esteemed as USC, that house is easily worth over $1,000,000 today. That was my introduction to the world of flipping houses.

THE START OF NOTHING BIG

Around 1992 or so, my step-grandfather convinced my dad to follow in his footsteps and learn the real estate business, so he obtained his real estate sales license. From my preface, you're probably thinking that I went on to become the son of a real estate mogul whose dad and grandad made millions flipping, buying, and selling real estate. Welp, sorry to inform you—that flip my dad and step-grandad did was the start of *nothing* big. They never did another flip deal even though money was made.

My dad kept his day job as an Electrician while brokering real estate deals as a side hustle with his father-in-law. Years later when I asked what they did with the money from the flip he laughed and said,

"I shoulda kept doing it, but we (he and my stepmom) spent the money instead. Damn shame!"

But hindsight is 20/20 for many of us. They didn't capitalize on it or reinvest the money to build their own real estate empire. They were younger and victims of capitalism like most of us when we come into lump sums of money we aren't accustomed to having. *Oh, how quickly can I spend it,* is the typical mindset.

After high school, I spent a year at San Diego State University and let me tell you, it was a *helluva party!* I wasn't ready and had no clear direction on what I wanted to do with my life at eighteen. Finance sounded good, so I declared it as a major. Unfortunately, instead of hitting the books, I exerted most of my energy chasing young women, drinking, and partying. My lazy and lax approach to college yielded nothing but letters from the University Dean initially putting me on notice of academic probation after my miserable first semester. The second notice was an official boot to my rear end, showing me the door. Yup, I was kicked out of college for my piss poor academic effort. Still, it was a *helluva party!*

It was the end of the summer of '92, following my failed college freshman year when I moved to Chicago with my biological mom. I spent the next four years working odd jobs, *courting* young ladies (as my paternal grandma once put it), club hopping round Chicago's Deep House scene, and chipping away at college credits here and there. Chicago turned out to be one *helluva party* too! Ahh, to be young, carefree, misguided, and undecided again.

It's funny how we never truly realize the impact some folks have on us. Every single person in my family (aunts, uncles, cousins, and grandparents) worked for a living. I never knew a businessperson in my family besides my maternal grandfather, but we weren't close. He lived in Chicago my whole life and I only saw him summers I'd visit as a kid. He was one of those street savvy, serial entrepreneurs who despised working for other people. Because of the distance between us, I never spent any time learning about business from him, but I remember visiting several establishments he owned throughout my young life—a multi-family building with a salon on the first floor, a gas station, and a car service.

He wasn't rich, but he kept money in his pocket and like the step-granddad and step-uncle I'd come to have, he didn't punch anyone else's clock! Perhaps all three of these men engrained a burning desire in me to become an entrepreneur just by their mere presence. How I'd accomplish this…I had no clue at 18, 19 or 20. I just knew and hoped that one day, someway—somehow, I would punch my own clock!

Do any of us really want to be relegated to what some company or corporation believes we're worth in the form of a paltry salary or hourly wage? In most of our minds we're worth much, much more than what we're paid, but accept the scraps because typically we have no other choice. Those bills keep on coming like clockwork and they are key components to keep us in the hamster wheel of life, trading time for money.

It's easier to settle for mediocrity than to push ourselves beyond the status quo. I suggest that you should work to pay your bills, but you should also build a business in your spare time so that it eventually replaces your j-o-b (just over broke), or at least supplements the cost of your lifestyle. I learned a long time ago that most people are okay with getting on the hamster wheel of life and not doing anything to attain the life they dream of. And this has nothing to do with money. Not everyone wants to be a millionaire, but damn, I know it felt good for my maternal grandfather, step-grandfather, and step-uncle to not have to check into someone's job every day. I would eventually come to know what that kind of freedom feels like.

On the other hand, if you like what you do, and it means working for someone else, keep doing it, but build something in your spare time. Hell, my dad genuinely liked being an Electrician. He worked hard to become a union journeyman and realized that real estate would be his side hustle to make a few extra dollars. And that is perfectly okay. However, the mindset of most folks was summed up in a quote I heard from motivational speaker, Myron Golden, *"Most people spend their free time entertaining themselves, while very few spend free time educating themselves or building a business."*

Let that quote sizzle in your spirit, then ask yourself where do you fit in? After working 8, 10, 12-hour shifts, do you sit down at the old idiot box (TV) and watch other folks living out their real, imagined, or scripted lives? Or do you pick up a book and learn something new that you can use to move the needle forward for yourself or your family? Do you do like I did for years; change clothes, and go to work for yourself after you punch out of the day job? Do you put in sweat equity with the hope that those long hours will one day bear fruit? You've heard this before; *we all get the same 24-hours in a day.* But what do you spend the most time doing? That is the difference between being mediocre and striving to move beyond mediocrity.

Don't get me wrong, we all need to unwind, unplug, and take in some entertainment every now and again, but if you are not where you want to be, not having experiences you long for, or the things you desire, then entertaining yourself should be kept to a minimum. I didn't intend for this chapter to be preachy or some kind of motivational speech but understand that flipping houses is a form of entrepreneurship that requires risk and work ethic. If you don't have the stomach for either, stick to your day job. You'll be doing yourself a huge favor. But if you want some firsthand nothing-to-something war stories, risk vs. reward, sweat equity and insider tips that you can use on your journey in the house flipping business, keep reading.

EFF YOU PAY ME!

Getting rich is not terribly hard once you know how, but staying rich can be challenging. What exactly does rich mean? It varies from person to person. For some it is a dollar amount; six, seven, eight figures or more. I attained a level of success in my life where I was able to retire my wife, walk away from my day job and support our household, but maintaining that life didn't last. I was a millionaire on paper if you tallied up the retail market value of all the properties I owned and I made close to $200K annually from these investments and I had stopped punching other people's clocks. Some would have called me rich. Perhaps, but I never felt that way inside.

In fact, the thing that sparked my drive or that fire in me to really chart a course to make it happen, was being denied a raise from my employer. I had been with my agency for probably seven or so years at the time, and of course being a government employee raises are few and far between, but I felt I deserved one, so I wrote a letter requesting an annual raise of about $8K - $10K and substantiating why I felt I deserved as much.

I suppose the Director pondered on my request for all of

five minutes, but she responded in writing a week or so later denying my request. It wasn't in their budget! Mind you, I had only gotten two or three raises over that seven-year period, so it was a huge slap in the face that made me furious. I wanted to quit, but I couldn't because I too was stuck on the hamster wheel. I felt devalued and insignificant. A couple of years earlier, when I reached five years on the job, I was given a pin to put on my lapel. They had me take a picture shaking hands with one of the Commissioners who also gave me a plaque signed by the Governor. *Fuck You, Pay Me,* is what I wanted to say. I kept my composure and said to myself, rewarding people with meaningless trinkets instead of cash is exactly how the system is designed to work; to exploit as much work out of folks while paying them as little as possible. And typically, only enough to keep them coming back day in and day out.

I thought back to a story my stepmom once told me about her brother who tried the corporate job routine as a young man but had either been fired or quit. The experience left him with a strong desire to never work for anyone else ever again. Lucky for him, he never did. In that moment as I pondered on being denied a paltry raise, I decided to build my own business so that I'd never have to worry about glass ceilings or asking for handouts ever again. It was a horrible feeling of not being able to control my own destiny. They didn't want to give me a raise? Well, I'd give myself my own damn raise!

If you read my first book about hard money lenders, you'd know that in 2008, after my wife was laid off and my real estate sales career went out the window with the real estate market meltdown of '07, I relocated from Los Angeles to Oklahoma City and established a real estate investment company. I did a flip, then paused for a few years to get my credit right, buy another residence and decide how to move forward. And after getting a big, fat middle finger in response to asking for a raise was just the spark I needed. It was time to put things back in motion.

Never afraid to invest in myself, I pulled some equity out of my primary residence to serve as seed money for executing my business plan. But just what was my plan? Well, I'll give you a couple of excerpts taken from my business plan at the time:

Mission

405 Homebuyers, LLC (company) is now being re-established as a property investing firm, including single-family homes and income producing multi-family dwellings.

The company operates out of its home office in Oklahoma City, OK, and is fully owned and controlled by Sean Danley, a full-time resident of Oklahoma City.

405 Homebuyers mission is to create investment income through the purchasing and reselling of distressed single-family residential property in Oklahoma County, OK for the purpose of rehabbing and reselling for profit to other investors and to owner occupants. Target properties will include REO foreclosures, pre-foreclosures, and potential short sales, all selling for well-below market value.

Financial Goals

405 Homebuyers will strive to create and maintain an image and reputation in the industry as an honest, cooperative, and creative enterprise, characterized by ethics, fair play, and win-win results. To ensure success, 405 Homebuyers will focus on the development of strong partnerships with key Real Estate professionals, i.e., sales brokers/agents, financial institutions, law firms, building trade contractors, real estate service firms, and others.

The company plans to purchase, rehab, and resell-for-profit a *minimum of 4 properties in its first year. With the experience gained in year one, the company expects to acquire and resell a minimum of 6 properties in year two and will continue to grow by at least 2 properties per year moving forward.*

As our experience grows, we expect to progressively move from lower-priced properties to higher-priced properties, where the profit margins will increase, allowing us to generate more income from the same number of projects.

In year one, the profit from each project is expected to average $15,000. In year two, as the company shifts towards tackling higher-end projects, we expect the average profit-per-project to increase to $20,000. In subsequent years, the projected profit-per-project should continue to rise, with the goal of increasing average profits by at least $5,000 per year.

I will confess that this business plan is well over ten years old as of the publication date of this book, but you'll want to have a plan before moving forward. As I explained in the HML book, potential lenders will want to see a business plan and they may even request you provide the following documents before even looking at a deal:

- Corporate registration documents and filings for your LLC, partnership, or corporation
- Operating Agreement
- Resolution
- Tax ID if you are not a sole proprietor (which you should not be for real estate investing)

You can find any number of free boilerplate templates for business plans, or you can pay to have one drafted by an attorney or company like Legal Zoom, etc. I chose the former and simply tweaked a lot of the information in Microsoft Word to fit my intended course of action.

Be mindful that your business plan is not set in stone and some of your goals and methods of execution may change. You'll want to remain agile in real estate. Try to revisit your plan periodically and tweak as needed, but certainly have a plan. The excerpts I provided certainly changed over time, but my ultimate goal of paying myself with real estate as the vehicle remained constant!

Your financial goals and profit margins will vary greatly depending on the market you operate in. I am in the Midwest where home values remain affordable, and we see less drastic appreciation than coastal cities like Los Angeles, New York, and Miami.

Again, this is from a plan I created over a decade ago, so my income forecast for the first five years of business looked like this:

Year	# of Projects	Average Profit	Total Annual Profit
1	4	$15,000	$60,000
2	6	$20,000	$120,000
3	8	$25,000	$200,000
4	10	$30,000	$300,000
5	12	$35,000	$420,000

So, you're probably wondering if I hit these numbers. Well, yes and no. I did end up owning twelve properties, but it took me less than five years. I never made $420,000 in a single year and that's not to say I couldn't have but let a public search of the website Buzzfile.com tell it, my former company (405 Homebuyers LLC's) gross annual income was just about $352,000 (see screenshot below). I have no clue where they came up with that figure. Like I said before, I hit close to $200K in my best year. Not bad for giving myself my own damn raise, huh?

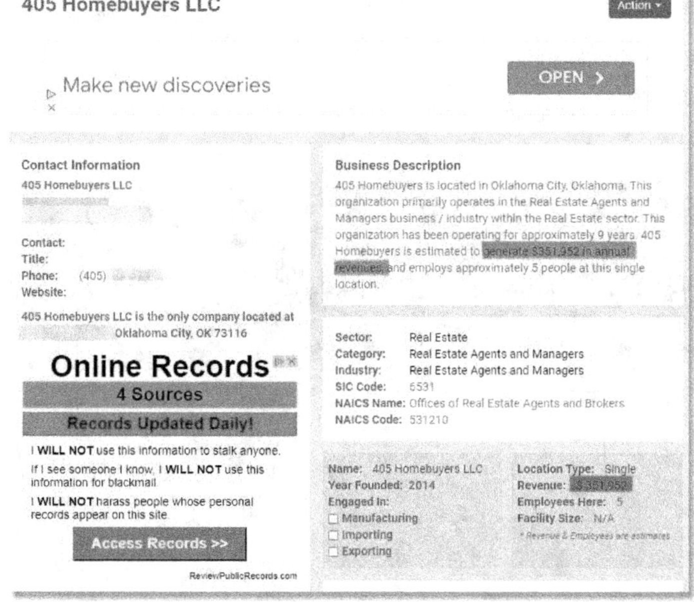

FLIPPING CRITERIA

The forecast numbers I laid out in the previous chapter are small in comparison to bigger coastal markets where property values are higher and can potentially yield greater returns. At some point before pulling the trigger on a flip, you'll have to decide what kind of properties you'll want to target. Also note that unless you've got a ton of cash or a blank check for buying properties, your lender will have specific criteria for properties they'll lend on; be it single-family homes, duplexes, triplexes or fourplexes. I've even run across lenders that will only lend purchase money and not rehab funds, so you'll want to come up with a strategy.

Perhaps you'll utilize different strategies to achieve both short and long-term financial goals. This might include a variety of property acquisition methods, a variety of renovation methods and a variety of disposing/selling methods, all dependent on the specific target property.

This was my strategy from my business plan:

Acquisition Strategies

The company intends to purchase distressed properties at or below 50% of fair market value. By purchasing properties at this far below market value, generating consistent and substantial profits will be achievable. Leveraging the depressed local real estate market, the company will focus on acquiring distressed single-family homes using a variety of means…

Was I always able to get properties at or below 50% after-repair market value? Nope, but 60–70% was not unusual. There always had to be an upside to any deal for it to make sense, meaning my goal was to force appreciation into as many properties as I could. This is very difficult to do with *pretty*, turnkey houses or those needing little to no work. With distressed homes needing serious TLC, it was possible to get those after-repair values up.

I could have easily made this chapter about funding your investment deals, but I already wrote a book about hard money lending, which may be your best bet if you don't have access to other resources like private money, the bank of mom and dad or you're lucky enough to be a trust fund-baby. If none of these apply, I suggest you pick up or download a copy of *"The Good and Bad About Hard Money Lenders"* on Amazon.

This chapter is about identifying your criteria for flip projects. It's a critical component because one size does not fit all. No different that when you are looking to purchase a residence, you can't just say to a real estate agent, "Hey, find me a house," right? No, you cannot. There must be context.

If you're going to be an active investor/flipper, I would suggest buying properties near where you live, so that you save time, money and gas visiting the properties you purchase. Even if you're not on-site every day, you'll want to be able to drop in and view the progress of the project.

Remember, it's your money or money you've borrowed at risk, so it's best to not be disconnected or hands-off. Furthermore, if you are just starting out, limited in resources, or just one of those folks who loves to get their hands dirty, you'll be putting in sweat equity. And you'll most likely be doing so outside of your day job, like I did at the beginning of my journey, so do yourself a favor and make it a 15 to 20-minute commute to your flip property instead of an hour or so drive home.

Here's what my target neighborhood criteria looked like:

Target Neighborhoods

405 Homebuyers, LLC will operate in the northeast and northwest corridor of Oklahoma County. These areas were chosen because of their significant population of homes in the company's target price range of $50,000 to $80,000 (remember this is 10 years old). Also, Sean has familiarity with those neighborhoods having lived and worked in the NW OKC area. In order to appeal to the widest audience of retail end buyers, these homes will be at least 3 bedrooms and 1.5 baths located on side streets close to schools, and inclusive of certain amenities which are desired by young, professional families.

I defined my target price range, number of bedrooms, bathrooms, and parts of town I would concentrate on. I will say that I did not limit the areas to just NW and NE OKC. I also bought several homes in SE OCK and Spencer, Oklahoma. And like I mentioned before, none of these areas were more than a 30-minute drive for me. Let's assume you will stick to single-family homes to flip, some other criteria you'll want to define is as follows:

- Size / square footage
- Style of property
- Age of property / year built
- Amenities

- Class of neighborhood

There is a reason sites like Zillow, Realtor and Redfin allow consumers to choose criteria in their quest for homes—because it matters. So, in addition to knowing your purchase price point, city, neighborhood, bed, and bathroom count, it's important to also know these other items I suggested.

Size or square footage is important for valuation or comparing to recent sales in the same area at purchase time and when you go to sell. Plus, you'll need these figures for purchasing renovation material (carpet, flooring, paint, HVAC systems, etc.). Most things are measured in square footage which directly affects your budget, so be very aware. I once read a horrible review of a hard money lender by a disgruntled investor who was upset that he was not allowed to extend a hard money loan a third time on a home that was some 4000 – 5000 SF in an affluent area. Turns out he couldn't flip the property as quickly as he thought. Well, flipping big expensive houses is much harder simply because your end buyers have much more capital and many more options like, let's say um, building their own custom homes. The investor didn't take that into account and probably thought he could do the Vanilla Ice Project thing.

The style of property you decide to flip is just as important. And I'll couple this with age of property because they should really be considered equally. I always steered clear of wood frame exterior houses and tried to avoid anything built before 1978—but not always. Some of these house-flipping TV shows only show the glamorous side of flipping, but not all the nuances and problems one can encounter. Why 1978? Well because in 1978, the federal government banned consumer use of lead-based paint in single-family homes, so any home you purchase or sell that was built before 1978 requires a lead-based paint disclosure that has to be completed by the seller and acknowledged by the buyer. So, when you go to renovate homes older than that and the paint is disturbed, lead based particles are released into the atmosphere, causing a potential health hazard.

Buying and renovating a ranch style home built in 1980 will be different than buying a 100-year-old Victorian home located in a historic neighborhood. The materials used to build the properties will vary significantly from plumbing to electrical. And you'll be limited to what you can change in a historic home by the neighborhood preservation society. You want to add a touch of modern to the old? Chances are red tape won't allow it.

I remember hearing of a new investor buying a century old property because it was *charming*. She wanted to bring it back to life. Remember I worked in the real estate industry for two decades and have come across and heard many horror stories. To make matters worse, she bought it without an inspection. Welp, once her contractor was able to get in to see the home after closing, she was told the place had knob and tube wiring throughout. And guess what? This was a *big, old house,* so it was going to cost her so much money on the electrical upgrade alone that she wanted to renege on the purchase. That was a matter for the courts to decide, which would have most likely cost her more money and not resulting favorably.

Amenities are not to be overlooked. I was a frequent attendee at my local real estate investor meeting once I took on the label of investor. As an introvert, I wasn't always heard, but I was seen. I wasn't big on small talk and chit-chat, but I passed out my card and took other people's business cards. I kept my conversations strictly business. Like they say, *your network is your net worth.*

One of the first things I did was I had several yard signs made with my company name, logo, phone number and "We Buy Homes" caption. I put a sign out front of every home I bought on the day I closed all the way through to selling or renting the home. I also posted a digital screenshot of the sign in my local Craigslist real estate section every week for exposure. Lastly, I made a flyer for every home I bought and emailed it to my investor network at purchase, sale and when I had a rental available. This way, your network knows you're in the game and serious about your business.

Do these things and your phone will ring with buyers, sellers and other investors looking to buy or sell you a deal. I had one investor in my network call me about a house he was sitting on but had no time to renovate, because he also owned and operated a roofing company. He asked me to go look and make him an offer if interested. When I arrived, the house met my criteria, but needed a full renovation. However, when I stepped into the backyard there was serious overgrowth and a pool that looked like the "Swamp Thing" might have lived there. Plus, there was a huge crack in the asphalt near the pool. I had to pass on the deal because although most people think of a pool as an awesome amenity and selling point, as an investor, it wasn't worth the headache. I would have had to drain it and lord knows what problems I may have uncovered after that. It probably just needed to be filled in, but not by me! So, be sure to evaluate amenities and your budget before buying an investment property.

The class of neighborhood is extremely important to evaluate because it will determine your exit strategy and end-buyer. Remember the guy who couldn't flip the 4000-plus square foot house in a class A neighborhood? He didn't do his homework and probably saw dollar signs.

Let's face it, rich folks have more options on where and what to spend their money on.

I stuck to buying homes in working class and lower-middle class (B to C-minus) areas where there may have been a mix of renters and homeowners. If I was going to flip the home, I needed it to be closer to a B class area. If I planned to rehab and hold it as an affordable housing unit, the area was typically C or C-minus.

Avoid investing in warzones or gang-infested areas if you can. Hey, but somebody's gotta do it. These areas will have the least or slowest property appreciation, although you can subsidize rents with government programs for steady cashflow—not to mention a host of other headaches. My next book installment will be entitled, "The Good and Bad About Section 8 Landlording," where I'll give you the rundown on my experiences as an affordable housing landlord.

Following a specific criterion for purchasing homes should be employed by all investors. Build a core competency in evaluating the condition of any potential purchase and what it will take to improve it appropriately. The level of renovation work for each property will depend on your exit strategy, ranging from big houses to little houses, newer or older houses, resale or renting, brick, stucco, wood-siding, etc., minor cosmetic improvements to major structural remodeling. Decide and move forward. You'll be glad you did.

LET'S MAKE A GOOD DEAL

The Good: real estate flipping gives you control over the process. When you flip a house, you have complete control over the process, from finding the property to making the renovations to selling it. This can be a great way to express your creativity and make a profit at the same time.

The Bad: real estate flipping requires patience and time commitment. You will need to find the property, make the renovations, and sell it. This can take several months or even years, but hopefully not the latter.

Making a *good* deal in real estate house flipping requires careful research, analysis, and negotiation skills. By understanding the market, conducting thorough research, and embracing the journey's challenges, you can navigate the world of real estate flipping with confidence. It demands patience, perseverance, and a willingness to weather the challenges that may arise along the way. However, with a well-thought-out plan, effective time management, and the ability to adapt to unforeseen circumstances, you can overcome the hurdles and ultimately achieve your desired goals.

Now that you've outlined your criteria, it's time to get a

good deal! Before you buy a house, make sure you research the neighborhood, the condition of the house, and the current market value of similar houses. Gain a deep understanding of the real estate market in the areas where you plan to invest. Analyze recent sales data, trends, and market conditions. Look for neighborhoods with high demand, potential for appreciation, and a history of successful flips. This will help you to identify undervalued properties that have the potential for a profit. You need to buy the house at a good price in order to make a profit when you sell.

Utilize various sources to identify undervalued properties with potential for profit. Look for distressed properties, foreclosures, or homes in need of significant repair. Go to foreclosure auctions, consult with real estate agents, or use online platforms to find off-market deals. One source you should definitely use is your County Assessor's web site. Here you should be able to find any address in your county with details on size, year built, property type, and sometimes even owner information, if disclosure is allowed. My home state of California does not publish owner names, whereas Oklahoma does.

A few popular online sources for finding sales information your target areas are "Zillow," "Realtor," or "Redfin" online databases. All these sources will be critical tools in your efforts to properly estimate the value of properties and determine the upside and downside potential of your flips. I would suggest using these sites for reviewing inventory currently on the market for sale and sold inventory. **DO NOT**—I repeat, **DO NOT** use Zillow for the values aka "Zestimate's" it places on properties. Most real estate professionals will tell you these Zestimate's are not reliable, and sometimes off by thousands of dollars. However, these sites do aggregate public data from the MLS and county records to provide accurate for sale and sold data.

Once you find a potential property, perform thorough due diligence. Research the property's history, including any liens or clouded title issues. The state in which you operate will determine whether a title company or attorney is used to close your transaction. Either way, having a relationship with a title attorney or title company can help you avoid properties tied up in litigation. Assess the condition of the house and estimate the cost of repairs and renovations. Consider hiring professionals such as home inspectors or contractors to evaluate the property thoroughly.

A rule of thumb I had as part of my due diligence process was to have all properties inspected by a licensed inspector or *trusted* contractor. I emphasize *trusted* because you don't want to be at the mercy of some fly-by-night, unscrupulous contractor you find on Craigslist or elsewhere. Unfortunately, there are tons of scam artists posing as contractors waiting for an *all-day sucker* to come along who they can take advantage of. Surround yourself with a team of professionals who can support your flipping venture. This may include real estate agents, contractors, inspectors, title agents and attorneys. Establishing a network of trusted individuals will help streamline the process and ensure smooth transactions.

Inspections provide a comprehensive checklist of property defects to be repaired during the renovation process. I always factored the cost of an inspection into each project, as part of the renovation costs. However, depending on the type of property you purchase and from whom (bank REO, auction, tough seller) inspections are not always allowed or no inspection contingency is allowed. This means that even if you find a defect of some sort, the seller will not credit you, reduce the sales price or offer any financial assistance toward any defect you find. You would simply agree to buy "as-is" or move on to another deal. I suggest that even if the seller requires you to buy the property "as-is," you should still have your contractor conduct a walkthrough with you to assess the condition of the property. Knowing what you must repair will make for better budgeting and planning.

CRUNCHING THE NUMBERS

Flipping houses isn't just about finding diamonds in the rough; it's about navigating a financial tightrope. In this chapter, we'll delve into the art of calculating renovation costs with precision and maximizing your profit on every flip.

The Good: real estate flipping has the *potential* for high profits. If you buy a property at a good price and renovate it well, you can make a significant profit when you sell it.

The Bad: real estate flipping comes with high risk. There is always the possibility that you will not be able to sell the property for a profit, or that you will lose money on the renovations. Also, you'll want to consult your tax professional, as you'll be taxed on short-term capital gains as opposed to long-term gains, which are typically more favorable for investors.

You'll want to utilize several resources to ensure that all renovations are evaluated and completed appropriately, on-budget, and on-schedule. I once had to fire a contractor for running too far behind on my timeline. He did great work, but just too slowly. More about that later.

Appraisals: Capture and review the sale prices of similar homes in your targeted neighborhoods over the past zero to six months (12 max) from three sources. You should have a relationship established with a reputable real estate sales professional with access to the Multi Listing Service (MLS) in your area. In my first book I talked about how I initially used an independent one-man shop, broker who setup auto-emailing of listings that matched my criteria. Just another reason to have your criteria identified. If you don't know what you're looking for, how will anyone else? This was a hassle-free way for me to set up showings for properties that piqued my interest.

Step 1: Assess the Scope of Work:

Walk the property and conduct a thorough inspection, noting cosmetic blemishes, structural issues, and outdated systems. Prioritize your to-do list by differentiating essential repairs from value-adding upgrades. Remember, every dollar spent will have an impact on your bottom line. Gather inspiration online and in-person. One of my favorite websites to visit for inspiration when I was flipping was Houzz.com. It's an online community and platform that showcases architecture, landscape, and interior design ideas. If you want a modern kitchen, a contemporary bathroom, a Fung Shui Zen-like backyard, or rustic feel, you will find inspiring ideas galore. You should also research local trends and popular finishes to understand buyer preferences in your target market. I became familiar with the work of several other flippers over time who had adopted sort of a signature style to their flips. If I saw a completely renovated home with fresh curb appeal and a modern red door, I knew exactly what investor had done the work.

Step 2: Calculate Your Numbers:

Evaluate the financial aspects of the deal carefully. Consider the purchase price, renovation costs, holding costs (such as mortgage payments, property taxes, and insurance), and selling costs (including real estate commissions and closing fees). Ensure that the projected expenses align with your desired profit margin.

The 70% Rule: This industry rule suggests limiting renovation costs to 70% of the After-Repair Value (ARV) minus the purchase price. While a starting point, adjust based on your project's specifics. I always liked a bit of a deeper discount where possible. If you plan on buying bank owned (REO) properties, just know that they are sticklers for pricing homes right at 70% discount depending on the condition, and typically no more than that. Also, don't expect any inspection contingencies when dealing with banks; you'll be buying "as-is."

Per-Square-Foot Method: Estimate costs based on average renovation costs per square foot in your region. Factor in quality variations and adjust for specific features like bathrooms or kitchens. Knowing your exit strategy up-front is a must. If you're flipping to maximize profits, modest finishes similar to or slightly better than those in the same vicinity are a must. If there are no comparable properties, make your flip the most updated property in the area, but don't break the bank or overdo it with ultra-high-end finishes that you won't be able to recoup in a sale.

I once bought a short-sale property to flip, wherein the owner was trying to get out from under the mortgage before the bank called the note due and began foreclosure proceedings. I knew the area well because I lived in the same community, just a few miles away. It was a 1970's brick home with all original finishes and décor. If nothing else, the neighborhood was desirable for young couples, first-time buyers, and even elderly folks. Most investors passed on the house because the inventory turnover was not as hot back then and they probably thought they couldn't price it high enough to get a decent return. But not me…

I knew that this house had good bones and because it was in an affordable, relatively quiet area that I could make it essentially the prettiest house on the block. Sometimes you have to take a chance and create the market you want. I turned that house completely around by upgrading every room, paint, hardware, flooring, bathroom and kitchen appliances and finishes, major mechanical systems, and interior and exterior paint. It became the prettiest house on the block and when it went up for sale, I got multiple offers right out the gate. I closed about 45 days later at an all-time high price for that area.

A few months later, a massive vacant lot just down the street from my flip broke ground on a new-construction subdivision with starting prices equal to my flip. You see, I took a chance and created an entire market, paving the way for home builders to take notice. That new home community was built to capacity soon after and sold out at prices far exceeding that of my flip.

Step 3: Mastering the Cost Breakdown:

Contractor Bids: Seek quotes from licensed contractors for complex projects or to validate your estimates. Get multiple bids and compare apples to apples.

Negotiate the Purchase: Armed with your research and financial calculations, negotiate with the seller to secure a favorable purchase price. Use your due diligence findings and market knowledge to justify your offer. Be prepared to walk away if the numbers don't work in your favor.

BALL OUT or BUDGET REHAB

By mastering the art of cost estimation and prioritizing smart spending, you'll navigate the financial aspects of flipping with confidence, maximizing your profits and turning fixer-uppers into financial successes. Whether you are a first time flipper or seasoned veteran of the game, you must continuously educate yourself about market trends, network with industry professionals, and learn from your experiences to refine your flipping strategies over time.

Each real estate flip is unique, and success requires a combination of market knowledge, due diligence, and calculated risk. Flipping houses is a dynamic dance between vision, sweat equity, and sometimes, strategic delegation. In this tango, contractors can be invaluable partners, but like any dance move, they require careful consideration before taking the floor. You are the CEO, whether you are a one man or one-woman shop; using sweat equity to complete your flips or outsource your rehab work to independent contractors.

You are the master of your checkbook, which means you control the money. Money that must be monitored, spent, reconciled, and more often than not, paid back to someone, some entity or a group of investors, if borrowing money to flip houses. My best advice is to be a good steward in this position. Once you prove that you are a good steward of investor funds and they see consistent returns, they'll be more than willing to open their checkbooks to you again and again.

First, having a budget and then deciding how you will use said budget to maximize profits while not skimping on quality is an artform all itself. As such, what you decide to do with a property begins long before you reach the closing table. Once you decide you're going to make an offer, the planning should begin to some degree. Remember, I suggested having a trusted contractor walk through the potential purchase with you beforehand? You should be able to get a rough estimate at that point. Once you get a few deals under your belt, you'll come to know how to estimate rehab costs on your own during a walk-thru. So, do you ball out or rehab on a budget? I suggest the latter, but it ultimately depends on your risk tolerance and exit strategy.

Consider using a licensed home improvement contractor who can oversee multiple trades, saving you time and streamlining communication. Successful flips often involve a strategic blend of do-it-yourself (DIY) and professional help. Choose your contractors wisely, and you'll have a smoother, more profitable dance towards your flipping goals. This can be a challenge, but most cities have a real estate investors association, so reach out to other local investors for referrals to quality contractors with a proven track record. I've seen some investors grow their business to the point where they were able to hire full-time staff to renovate their flip projects and maintain their rental properties.

If you're just starting out you may not have the financial means to hire contractors, so you're left to do the work yourself or with the help of friends and family perhaps. But, unless you are some DIY junkie who loves getting their hands dirty, this is a slow, time-consuming and arduous approach. What is your time worth? You will come to realize that your time could be best spent looking for more deals and driving around inspecting your rehab rather than actually doing the work it takes to complete a rehab. For me, sweat equity got old quickly. Besides, unless you are a former carpenter or trade professional, hire the professionals to do what they do best. You may spend a bit more money, but you'll save *big time* on time and costly mistakes or plain old subpar DIY workmanship.

Ultimately, the decision to hire contractors hinges on your project's scope, your own expertise, and your risk tolerance. Consider your individual strengths and weaknesses, the complexity of the flip, and your budget before making a decision. But if you do, do your due diligence. There are too many horror stories out there about fly-by-night contractors, who duped some unsuspecting client out of thousands of dollars and either never performed or did substandard work.

During the renovation phase, closely monitor the expenses to stay within your budget. Regularly communicate with contractors, track costs, and make necessary adjustments to avoid cost overruns. Efficient project management can contribute significantly to the overall profitability of the flip. Accuracy is key. Overestimating costs leads to missed opportunities, while underestimating can derail your entire project. Consider using online renovation cost calculators and consult experienced flippers for guidance.

Material costs, labor costs, permits, and waste disposal fees should all be line items in your budget. Research material options and negotiate with suppliers for bulk discounts. Setup accounts at big box stores like Home Depot and Lowes to take advantage of these discounts when you buy in bulk. For example, if you're flipping a house, you'll certainly want to change all the locks, so you can buy packs of door hardware and benefit from the cost savings. I started making so many trips to these retailers that the cashiers knew me by name. Indirect costs like holding costs (mortgage payments, taxes, insurance), realtor fees, staging, and closing costs should also be factored into your ARV calculations. And lastly, hidden costs, like unexpected repairs, delays, and potential overruns should be expected and taken into account with a contingency buffer of 10-15% of your budget.

Maximize profitability with value engineering. Value engineering suggests you seek cost-effective alternatives without compromising quality. Choose laminate flooring over hardwood or shaker cabinets over custom-built. Some flippers want to follow the latest and greatest décor trends and materials. I remember when folks started choosing quartz over marble countertops, but it was a bit more pricey. But I flipped in the realm of average 3-BR family homes in working class neighborhoods; not-ultra high-end for a very good reason.

High end flips can take forever to sell. Folks with more money can be very picky or even custom build. So, if you think you're going to make a killing flipping a distressed mini manse in some upscale neighborhood, it could take you months to sell if not an entire year. I've seen it many times over, even to the point where the flipper runs out of money and gives up mid-rehab. Don't let that be you. There is a much greater pool of buyers looking for updated homes in modest, working-class areas than upper-high class areas. As I passed by some rehab projects in high-end areas that seemed to take forever to complete or sell, I was the investor driving by wondering, "Wow, how much money are they losing on carrying costs?"

As I stated before, I don't suggest the sweat equity route, because I've been there and done that. Honestly, it taught me more about what I should not be attempting than anything. However, you may consider tackling simple tasks yourself if your skills allow. I happened to have experience in the plumbing trade, so I would tackle minor tasks like installing angle stops, plumbing fixtures or an occasional water heater. Painting, light demolition work, and landscaping yourself can save money, but estimate your time, experience level and quality of the finished product before taking on any such task.

Another cost savings is to smart source, which means to explore salvage yards, discount retailers, and online marketplaces for deals on materials without sacrificing quality. I did this often, but it had its drawbacks. For example, I would regularly visit my local Renovation Station stores during a project. Builders often donate their leftover materials (paint, flooring, etc.) from large projects, which you can purchase at a fairly decent discount. The only problem is they may not have enough material to meet your project needs. The quantities they have on the showroom floor are usually all there is, and it will be hard to know where it came from and how to match if you need more. Also, all sales are final, so don't try to color match paint when buying from this type of reseller.

Optimize the timeline and minimize holding costs by streamlining the renovation process. Plan efficiently, manage contractors effectively, and anticipate potential delays. I told you that I had to fire a contractor, not because he did poor work, but because he moved at a turtle's pace and would bring in help somedays and not others. This slowed down my timeline, so he had to go. I hired a crew of four guys that did quality work and finished the job in a timely manner.

DEAL AIN'T DONE UNTIL IT FUNDS

So, you've completed your first or maybe your fifteenth flip. You've accepted a full-price offer and you're headed to the closing table in about 30 days. Well, don't pop the bubbly or start spending money that hasn't hit your bank account just yet. I was offered some great advice by my broker in my early days of selling real estate back home in Los Angeles—*the deal ain't done until it funds!* Waiting until closing is crucial when it comes to flipping houses. In the fast-paced world of house flipping, it's tempting to celebrate a signed contract with high fives and champagne bottle poppin'. I prefer sparkling apple cider but hold your horses! In this real estate game, closing is king, and celebrating prematurely can lead to heartbreak and financial loss.

Thankfully, I learned that lesson long before I entered the world of house flipping. I usually don't release a sigh of relief until the deal has funded, not just closed. What's the difference you ask? Well, closing occurs at the title company or closing attorney's office where the buyer comes in to sign all docs and then the seller or vice-versa.

At that moment, all the paperwork associated with the transaction should be completed, but there can often be hiccups even at the eleventh hour that cause the deal to fall through. Real estate transactions are intricate, involving inspections, appraisals, and financing approvals. Any of these hurdles can derail the deal, even after the contract is signed. Celebrating too early sets you up for emotional disappointment and wasted effort if the deal falls apart. However, once the deal funds that means all requirements have been met and the funds are transferred/wired to the appropriate parties. The transaction is then recorded in the county record. Only then is it time to celebrate.

When I was a struggling real estate salesperson, I had a listing that was headed to closing. It had passed inspections; the appraisal was good, and the buyer was fully qualified with a rate lock. A day before the scheduled closing or 24-hours before I was to collect my commission check, I got a call from the buyer's agent who proceeded to tell me that her buyer's lender was pulling the loan and we would not be closing. *What the fuuuuu????* Yes, that's what I thought to myself as she went on to explain that her buyer, thinking the deal was as good as gold, went out and purchased a new car—before closing! This was obviously due to the mortgage broker and/or the agent's lack of experience because they should have explicitly told the buyer not to make any new purchases that would affect her debt-to-income ratio. Well, her car shopping fiasco cost her a nice, new house, but I hope the car was worth it! I'm pretty sure it wasn't.

Because of the hot real estate market in Los Angeles at the time, I had the property relisted and sold about 45 days later. But this is just one example of the types of things that can happen at the last minute, so be prepared. Other factors that can derail the closing process include liens or title issues that can surface last minute. Budgeting accurately is crucial, and celebrating before knowing your final expenses can lead to financial strain. I once bought a property from a woman that I kept as a rental, and while everything seemed straightforward, what should have been an *easy peasy*, quick closing ended up delayed for about 2 months while she hired an attorney to perform a quiet title action on the property. Turns out, she owned the property with her deceased sister without the right to survivorship. Therefore, she could not simply transfer the title to another party. I could have easily walked away from the deal, but by that time I was flipping and land lording on all cylinders, so I could afford to wait two months to close. However, because the house was vacant, I asked the owner for early occupancy, so I could start the cleanout and prep work for the rehab. Of course, I did this with assurances that the quiet title action would be resolved, and I wouldn't be wasting my time, money, and resources.

Legally, the property isn't yours until closing, so premature celebrations can create confusion and complicate matters if legal issues like the examples above arise before closing. Focus on ensuring a smooth closing first, then celebrate with peace of mind. The housing market is dynamic. Between signing and closing, unforeseen events like interest rate hikes or economic downturns can impact the property's value. Remember that flipping houses is a business, and emotions can cloud judgment. Homeowners carry emotions into real estate deals. Investors carry calculators and only numbers matter! Waiting until the deal funds shows professionalism, protects your finances, and allows you to celebrate a guaranteed success. You'll undoubtedly find ways to celebrate successful closings. I used to take my wife or wife and kids out to dinner as a celebratory gesture. But then it was onto the next deal. Now go out there and get those deals done!

ABOUT THE AUTHOR

Sean T. Danley is a former real estate salesperson and broker who established real estate investment companies 405 Homebuyers and 405 Rentals and Investors Realty in OKC, where he flipped single-family homes and grew a rental property portfolio valued at over $1,000,000. For a decade, he also served as a Real Estate Industry Regulator. Sean authored the book, "The Good & Bad about Hard Money Lenders" to help dispel myths surrounding the use of hard money as part of the investment strategy.